2-

MARISSA
MEYER

MARISSA MEYER

LAURA LA BELLA

ROSEN
PUBLISHING®

New York

Published in 2016 by The Rosen Publishing Group, Inc.
29 East 21st Street, New York, NY 10010

First Edition

Library of Congress Cataloging-in-Publication Data

La Bella, Laura.
Marissa Meyer/Laura La Bella.—First edition.
    pages cm.—(All about the author)
Includes bibliographical references and index.
ISBN 978-1-4994-6278-4 (library bound)
1. Meyer, Marissa—Juvenile literature. 2. Authors, American—21st century—Biography—Juvenile literature. 3. Young adult fiction—Authorship—Juvenile literature. I. Title.
PS3613.E974Z56 2016
813'.6—dc23
[B]
                                        2015024383

Manufactured in China

CONTENTS

Glass slippers, poisonous apples, a charming prince, an evil stepmother, wicked witches and a big bad wolf . . . mix these iconic fairy tale elements with mechanical feet, cyborgs, satellites hovering high above earth, computer hackers, and a queen who will stop at nothing for world domination and you have the mesmerizing universe of the Lunar Chronicles.

The *New York Times* best-selling series has been called "spellbinding" by *VOYA Magazine*, "ambitious, wholly satisfying" by *Publishers Weekly*, "absorbing" by *BCCB*, and "completely enjoyable" by *Bookshelves of Doom*. And it all comes from the creative mind of author Marissa Meyer.

Meyer has taken classic fairy tales and given them a science fiction spin. After honing her writing skills with fan fiction in high school, Meyer took an idea she created from a writing contest she had entered and turned it into an alternate universe of science fiction, fairy tale and fantasy. The Lunar Chronicles' four novels—*Cinder*, *Scarlet*, *Cress* and *Winter*—are all based on individual fairy tales (*Cinderella*, *Little Red Riding Hood*, *Rapunzel* and *Snow White and the Seven Dwarfs*, respectively) but are interwoven in a way that connects the main characters to an overarching story of love and betrayal and friendship

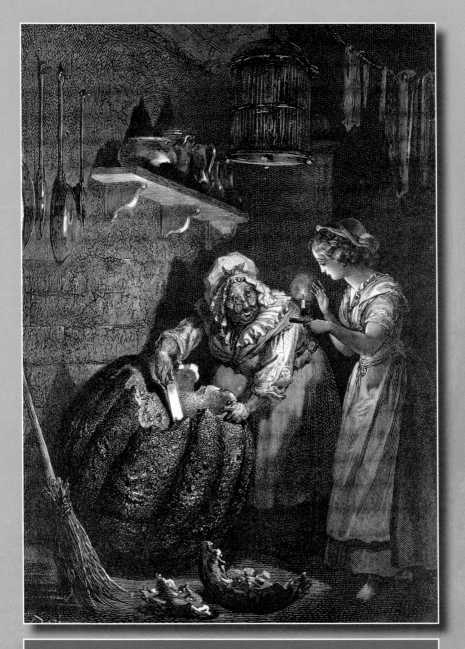

The story of Cinderella is a well-known folk tale. Thousands of iterations have been written around the world. *Cinder*, Marissa Meyer's first novel, is a high-tech version of the classic story.

and loyalty set against a world of technology and innovation.

The initial idea for *Cinder*, the first novel of the Lunar Chronicles, came from a dream Meyer had of Cinderella as a cyborg. Curious about where this story could go, Meyer registered for National Novel Writing Month, or NaNoWriMo, and spent the month of November 2010 crafting her story. The result was not only a rough draft of *Cinder*, but more than 80,000 words of text that would eventually become the basis for *Scarlet* and *Cress*, books two and three of the series.

After securing an agent, Meyer, with a full manuscript in hand and summaries of her next three novels, began pitching publishing houses. With an unprecedented offer from a publishing house to an author with no previous publishing experience, Meyer sold the Lunar Chronicles to Macmillan Publisher's Feiwel and Friends.

Cinder was released on January 3, 2012. In its first week it debuted at #10 on the *New York Times* best-seller list. Each of Meyer's subsequent novels in the series, plus *Fairest: Levana's Story*, a companion novel that reveals the backstory of the series' evil queen, have all debuted on the *New York Times* best-seller list upon release.

With the Lunar Chronicles series wrapped up, Meyer has begun to expand her writing to include new stories, all within her unique genre of science fiction and fairy tale. *Heartless* tells the story of a young Queen of Hearts from *Alice in Wonderland* and in development is a potential series about superheroes.

Meyer's blend of science fiction, fantasy and fairy tale has won the hearts of millions of readers who, across the world, have fallen in love with their favorite fairy tales in an exciting, new way.

ONE

CHAPTER

A FASCINATION WITH FAIRY TALES

Marissa Meyer was born on February 19, 1984, in Tacoma, Washington. Like many young girls at the time, Meyer was introduced to fairy tales through movies and storybooks. The first movie she ever saw in a theater, at age five, was Disney's *The Little Mermaid.*

"I was raised on Disney movies, like most of my generation," Meyer said in an interview with TeenReads.com, a website that provides reviews of young adult novels, excerpts of new releases, and author profiles. "But I was still really young when I was given a book of fairy tales that had Hans Christian Andersen's 'The Little Mermaid' in it, and I remember being shocked at how different it was from the Disney movie. It really made me question

The Little Mermaid statue, located in Copenhagen, Denmark, is a major tourist destination. It's based on the fairy tale of the same name by Danish author Hans Christian Andersen.

how other popular fairy tales might be different from the movies I was familiar with, and that kicked off a fascination that I have to this day."

That fascination only grew as Meyer began attending science fiction conventions and Renaissance fairs with her parents. She loved dressing up and would often attend these events in the costumes of her favorite characters, from Maid Marian (*Robin Hood*) and Princess Leia (*Star Wars*) to a Klingon (*Star Trek*). She told *USA Today*, "I have lots of pictures of me dressed up that had nothing to do with Halloween!"

But her discovery of the "Disney discrepancy" turned her toward the works of both Andersen and the Brothers Grimm. By reading many of these famous texts, Meyer soon learned that Disney's retelling of fairy tales was much more romanticized, and much less violent. In the Grimm Brother's version of *Cinderella*, when the stepsisters try on the glass slipper at the end of the story, they each cut off a toe or a heel in an attempt to make the shoe fit. Meyer found herself shocked by the significant differences.

As a teen Meyer also was into reading works by some of the great writers who have made careers out of retelling classic fairy tales in new ways. Among her favorites are Gail Carson Levine and Shannon Hale. Levine is best known for writing *Ella*

Enchanted, a retelling of Cinderella that was turned into a successful feature film in 2004 that starred Oscar-winning actress Anne Hathaway. Hale had success with the *Princess Academy* and the *Ever After High* series.

ALWAYS TELLING STORIES

Meyer loved to tell stories and was always reading during her childhood. Among her favorites books are J.R.R. Tolkien's *The Hobbit,* C.S. Lewis's *The Chronicles of Narnia series,* and R.L. Stine's *Goosebumps* series. "I grew up telling stories, and was constantly lost in a daydream. When I realized that writing was a real occupation, I knew immediately that's what I wanted to do with my life," Meyer said in an interview

J. R. R. Tolkein, author of the best-selling fantasy novels *The Hobbit* and *The Lord of the Rings* trilogy, is among Marissa Meyer's favorite authors.

with *VOYA Magazine*. "That said, I had an English teacher in tenth grade who read the start of a novel I was working on and told me she thought I could get it published someday. Which seems silly looking back—it was my first novel attempt—but I always appreciated those words."

DISCOVERING FAN FICTION

While in ninth grade, Meyer became an avid fan of *Sailor Moon*, a Japanese shōjo manga series written and illustrated by Naoko Takeuchi. Manga are Japanese comics that use a wide range of storytelling genres, or types, that include action-adventure, romance, historical drama, comedy, drama, science fiction, and fantasy. Shōjo manga is manga marketed to young girls between the ages of 10 and 18. *Sailor Moon* was among the most popular shōjo manga series of the mid-1990s. The series follows the adventures of Usagi Tsukino, a middle school student who is given the power to transform into a magical alter ego named Sailor Moon. Joined by other Sailor Soldiers, the name given to a group of young girls who have had their powers awakened, Usagi defends the planet against an assortment of evil villains. The popularity of the *Sailor Moon* story led to three films, thirty-nine video games, and a number of soundtracks. For Meyer, it was a story that combined many of her interests, including science fiction, fairy tales, action adventure and romance.

When Meyer was in ninth grade she discovered *Sailor Moon* fan fiction online. Fan fiction includes many kinds of works, from fictional stories and graphic art to videos or illustrations, that are inspired by a book, film, or TV show. This content is created by fans of the original piece of work and most commonly published to a fan fiction website for other fans or fan fiction creators to read. Fan fiction can take many shapes. Some fans write fan fiction to continue a beloved story, picking up where the original story ends and adding new plots and even the introduction of additional characters. Other fan fiction includes the retelling of the original story in a new way. Many popular novels, including those in *The Twilight Saga* by Stephanie Meyers and the *Harry Potter* series by J.K. Rowling, have large bases of fan fiction with several hundreds of thousands of fan fiction stories. Fans can post their work to a range of websites where others can read and comment on the work.

Meyer began writing *Sailor Moon* fan fiction

The 2013 New York Comic-Con is shown here. Meyer and her parents would dress in costume to attend similar events, where science fiction, comic book, and fantasy fans gather.

under the pen name Alicia Blade. "I remember writing my first fanfic in math class and my friends passing it around during lunch and encouraging me to post it online, which I did," Meyer told VoyaMagazine.com in an interview. "It was my first time sharing anything I wrote with strangers." Meyer wrote more than 40 fan fiction stories based on *Sailor Moon*.

COLLEGE BOUND

After graduating from high school, Meyer attended Pacific Lutheran University, which is located in Tacoma, her hometown. Here she majored in creative writing and minored in children's literature. Meyer was able to boost her knowledge of fairy tales through a variety of courses, including one called "Fairy Tale and Fantasy Literature." In an interview with Teenreads.com, Meyer said the course examined "the psychology and symbolism behind fairy tales. How certain elements are like a 'code,' hinting at things like social unrest, sexual maturation, religion and morals, etc." The class taught her that fairy tales were more than damsels in distress, handsome princes and happily ever afters. Meyer's perception of fairy tales was forever

altered. She told Teenreads.com, "though I can still read and appreciate a fairy tale as a children's story

Meyer was born and raised in Tacoma, Washington, attended college there, and after earning a master's degree on the East Coast, returned to the city to get married and raise her family.

without trying to pick it apart, I'll never be able to read them exactly the same way again."

After completing her bachelor's degree in 2007, Meyer continued her education at Pace University in New York City, where she earned a master's degree in publishing. When she graduated from Pace, Meyer returned to Washington state and worked as an editor for a publishing company for five years before leaving the world of publishing to become a freelance typesetter and proofreader.

MEYER'S FAN FICTION LAUNCHES A WRITING CAREER

While she was in college and throughout her early professional life, Meyer continued to write fan fiction, under the name Alicia Blade. In an interview with *The News-Tribune*, a daily newspaper in Tacoma, Meyer said writing fan fiction helped her learn the craft of writing, gave her instant feedback on her work, and taught her how to take criticism.

Interested in seeing where her writing could take her, Meyer entered a writing contest online where the host invited writers to craft a story by selecting from a list of ten prompts, or ideas. Each

FIVE MOST POPULAR FAN FICTION WEBSITES

Online fan fiction writing sites are depositories where fans can post their original writing and receive feedback. On many sites you need to become a member, often by registering for free, before you can read and/or comment on entries submitted by others. The following fan fiction websites are among the most popular. These are general interest websites that encompass a wide range of fan fiction topics.

FanFiction.net – Considered to be world's largest collection of fan fiction. The site has more than two million users who post fan fiction in more than 30 languages.

Quotev.com – A website where users can share fan fiction stories, serialized novels, quizzes, polls, and surveys.

KindleWorlds.com – Created by the online store Amazon, KindleWorlds allows fan fiction authors to earn money on the stories they write. Fan Fiction works are fully-fledged ebooks and are sold in the Kindle Store, just like other Kindle titles.

WattPad – Based in Toronto, Canada, Wattpad is one of the largest book communities on the Web, and one of the largest sources of free reads. It hosts a monthly audience of more than ten million readers.

The Archive of Our Own (archiveofourown. com) is a project founded and operated by the Organization for Transformative Works, a non-profit, non-commercial archive for all formats of fan fiction, including writings, graphic art, videos, and podcasts.

writer had to include at least two of the predetermined ideas in their story. Meyer chose two prompts: to set the story in the future and include at least one fairy tale character. The result was a futuristic version of *Puss in Boots*, a fairy tale about a cat who uses trickery and deceit to gain power and wealth. A version of the Puss in Boots character was made famous in the *Shrek* movies.

While she didn't win the writing contest, Meyer did begin to think about how she might retell some of her favorite fairy tales and she began brainstorming ideas for future writing projects. While drifting off to sleep one night she began to think about Cinderella. "One night, I had a dream about Cinderella. She tripped on the palace steps, but instead of her glass slipper falling off, her whole foot fell off. When I woke up, I thought to myself, 'her foot fell off because she's a cyborg.' For the first time I felt like I had landed on something that I had to write," Meyer told the *Mooring Mast*, the student-run newspaper of Pacific Lutheran University. Meyer jumped out of bed and began writing down ideas for a story about Cinderella as a cyborg. She became excited about putting a new spin on these beloved tales from childhood. These initial ideas would eventually become a first draft of her debut novel, *Cinder*.

MEYER'S FAMILY LIFE

Meyer is married to Jesse Taylor and the couple are parents to three cats named Calexandria Josephine, Blackland Rockwell III and Stormus Enormous. In December 2014, Meyer and her husband became foster parents to two babies. While the couple has kept details of their foster children closely guarded, Meyer did write in her blog, hosted on her website (marissameyer.com), that they hope to adopt both of the children in the future.

CHAPTER TWO

A WRITING CAREER TAKES SHAPE

As Meyer began to create a world for a young cyborg Cinderella, she revisited the science fiction books, TV shows, and films she loved when she was growing up. She soon realized that within these worlds of advanced technology it is the heart of the characters she connected with most. "My favorite sci-fi stories are *Star Wars* and *Firefly*, which are science-fiction, there's alien planets, technology, and spaceships, but they're really about the characters. I feel like that's how I kind of got into sci-fi, thinking it's not about the technology or language, it's about the people," she told BiblioFriend.com in an interview.

With characters and plot ideas in mind, Meyer needed both the opportunity and the motivation to begin fleshing out a fuller story for her novel. She decided to take advantage of National Novel Writing Month's one-month novel writing challenge.

Meyer counts *Firefly* among her favorite shows. Cast members Nathan Fillion, writer/director Joss Whedon, actress Summer Glau, and actor Sean Maher answer questions on a panel for the show's tenth anniversary.

ONE MONTH LEADS TO DRAFTS OF THREE NOVELS

Meyer decided to dedicate herself to writing a full first draft of *Cinder* by registering for National Novel Writing Month, or NaNoWriMo, a one-month writing challenge held annually during the month of November. Established as a nonprofit organization in 1999, National Novel Writing Month hosts NaNoWriMo, an event where participants are encouraged to work toward writing a 50,000-word novel in thirty-one days. The goal at the end of the month is not a polished, final draft of a novel, but instead a first draft of a project that writers can further build upon. Using the site's (nanowrimo.org) resources, which include blog

Marissa Meyer used National Novel Writing Month (NaNoWriMo) as a catalyst to produce a working draft of her first novel. Here, a group of writers participate in NaNoWriMo in a Washington, D.C., bookstore café.

posts and pep talks from published authors, inspiring ideas, advice, and a writing community to find support and encouragement, NaNoWriMo writers can track their progress and support one another during the challenge.

In interviews, Meyer has frequently talked about how valuable the NaNoWriMo experience was in helping her draft *Cinder*. She told BiblioFriend: "I think a lot of writers are inspired by NaNoWriMo. I think for many first writers or aspiring writers it can really be a struggle to finish that first book. NaNoWriMo encourages you to just write and not care about how good it is and just get something finished, just get something on the page. I think that helps a lot of writers get over that first hurdle. Once you've finished the book, you have something there you can revise and work with. It also shows you that you're capable of finishing something. I think it's a great program that has inspired a lot of people."

As Meyer began her month of writing, she soon found herself thinking of more than one story. In addition to a retelling of *Cinderella*, Meyer began brainstorming ideas for additional novels. Over the course of the month, Meyer wrote more than 150,000 words. Her first draft of *Cinder* was 70,000 words and the remaining 80,000 words became first drafts of *Scarlet* and *Cress*, books that would become the second and third novels of a larger series. Of her first drafts, Meyer told *The News Tribune*: "They were horrible, of course, because they were written in a month, but I really loved the concept and I thought they had so much potential."

Once the month came to an end, Meyer set her novels aside. Over the course of several months, Meyer returned to her manuscript for *Cinder* to further write, edit and revise the story. Two years later she produced a final draft.

MEYER'S WRITING PROCESS

Meyer likes to write both at home and at a café near Pacific Lutheran University, where she went to college. Being away from her house allows her to escape the household chores that distract her from writing. "There's dishes in the sink and laundry piling up. You just need to get out and focus," Meyer said in an interview with *The News Tribune*.

As Meyer wrote *Cinder* she began to develop her own writing process, which ended up being a nine-step process that suited the complexity of her novels as well as their originality. Detailed on her blog (http://www.marissameyer.com/blog), Meyer has been forthcoming about her writing process, how she manages the editing and revision process, and how much work goes into each of her novels.

BEST-SELLING NOVELS THAT STARTED DURING NANOWRIMO4

Since its in formation in 1999, more than 320,000 people annually participate in National Novel Writing Month. Several popular novels got their start as drafts created during NaNoWriMo, including the following titles, all of which have spent time on the *New York Times* best-seller list.

Water for Elephants by Sara Gruen is the story of veterinary student Jacob Jankowski, who leaves school and finds himself aboard a circus train, where he takes a job as an animal caretaker and falls in love with a circus performer.

The Night Circus by Erin Morgenstern is set in a wandering mystical circus that magically appears in empty fields across the world and is only open from sunset to sunrise. Within this night circus, romance and deception mix with love and magic as two performers engage in a competition neither truly understands.

Fangirl by Rainbow Rowell follows the lives of two very different sisters as they leave for college. One, a lonely writer of fan fiction, the other an outgoing social butterfly, each find their way amid college life, new friends, boys and the disjointed family they left behind.

Several best-selling novels began as NaNoWriMo projects, including *Fangirl*, by Rainbow Rowell. Here, Rowell appears on stage during the children's book and author breakfast at the 2015 BookExpo America.

Wool by Hugh Howey is a self-published e-book phenomenon of a society that exists in a giant silo underground, hundreds of stories deep. When one member of the community asks to go outside it leads to a drastic chain of events.

The Darwin Elevator by Jason M. Hough is set in the mid-twenty-third century and Darwin, Australia, is the last human city on Earth. It's the only place safe from the alien plague that destroyed the rest of humanity.

STEP 1: BRAINSTORMING AND RESEARCH

Because so many iterations of fairy tales exist, it would have been easy for Meyer to duplicate another plot line as she developed *Cinder*. To avoid this, she begins her writing process by brainstorming ideas and conducting research.

Meyer keeps an active list of story ideas, plot lines, or even scenes that constantly pop into her head. Like many writers, Meyer has ideas that won't ever be developed into a piece of writing, but once one of her ideas grabs her she begins a thorough and thoughtful research process. That process begins with Meyer asking herself questions to further develop an idea. Who is the protagonist? What is the main conflict of the story? Who are the other characters? Where does the story take place? These questions all help Meyer determine the plot of her story and help her flesh out a fuller idea of what the story is about. Once she has some initial information jotted down, usually by hand in a notebook, Meyer begins doing factual research for a book.

For *Cinder*, the factual research for her futuristic world began with Meyer reading countless issues of *Scientific American,* a popular science magazine that explores both current and emerging research and developments in the worlds of science, space

Building on her initial idea of a cyborg character based on Cinderella, Meyer's research further cemented her effort to bring her science fiction/fairy tale hybrid, *Cinder*, to life.

and technology. The magazine helped to build Meyer's knowledge of technology and the technological advancements that were currently in development that she could realistically portray in her futuristic world. While developing the setting for *Cinder*, which takes place in New Beijing, China, Meyer pored over Chinese travel guides to gain a better understanding of the culture and customs of the country, as well as to gain information on particular destinations she wanted to use as settings in the book. She used Google Street View to "walk" the streets of Paris, France, so she could virtually "see" the city's layout without having to travel there. This enabled Meyer to write more accurate descriptions of scenes that take place in Paris in book two, *Scarlet*. Meyer completes her research

The action in *Scarlet* begins in a quiet farming community in Rieux, France, and eventually makes its way to Paris. Technology helped Meyer envision her foreign settings before she ever had the chance to visit the French capital.

to gather information she might use in the story, as well as to develop various plot points.

STEP 2: CREATING AN OUTLINE

Once Meyer has concluded the research and brainstorming portion of her process, she begins to outline the plot of her story. Meyer reviews all of her research, especially any scene ideas she has developed, and begins ordering them based on what she feels is the beginning, the middle and end of the story. As she writes, Meyer knows the story will go in directions she doesn't anticipate. But her outline serves as an anchor for the story. Meyer said in her blog, "I don't follow my outline to the letter. The story inevitably takes on a life of its own, and I just try to keep up. But when I feel like the story is losing its way, I have that original roadmap to fall back on. I might take an occasional detour, but I can always look back and see where I was heading in the first place."

STEP 3: THE FIRST DRAFT

With an outline in hand, Meyer works quickly to write a first draft. In general, Meyer writes 3,000 to 6,000 words per day and never rereads previous chapters. She makes it a point to constantly move forward with the story until she reaches the end. Meyer approaches her first draft with a strategy: She sets a daily word goal, she fills her first draft with random notes about plot points or other ideas she will reference later, she keeps moving forward, she skips around when she gets stuck, and, most importantly, she keeps writing. The first draft is her favorite part of her writing process. On her blog she wrote: "The first draft … there's so much that could happen. So many surprises await you! So many twists and mysteries to be uncovered! So many characters to fall in love with!"

STEP 4: TAKING A BREAK

Once Meyer finishes a first draft she puts it aside and takes a long break. She lets her mind rest from the intensive writing required to produce a lengthy draft in a short period of time. She will often use the break to work on something else. "I reach a point in every book where I start to hate it a little bit. (I've come to find that all writers feel this way from time to time, so I've stopped feeling guilty about it.) Writing is hard. Books are difficult. You're not always going to be in that happy honeymoon period. But if I can set a book aside for a while and forget whatever was driving me crazy about it, when I return it's like rediscovering a past love," Meyer wrote on her blog.

STEP 5: THE SECOND DRAFT

This is the draft when Meyer begins revising her story. The plot thickens, the details begin to link together, and the story's direction becomes clear. Meyer uploads her first draft into Scrivener, a word processing software application that aids in the editing of longer documents like manuscripts. She then reads through the first draft over the course of a day or two. She isn't doing major rewriting at this point. Instead, she's getting a sense of the big picture. She marks places where she needs to fix something and keeps a running list of major changes she wants to make. These changes can consist of complete rewrites to a chapter, holes in the plot that need to be filled in, or characters or relationships that need to be better defined.

For example, in the first draft of *Scarlet,* Wolf had amnesia. As Meyer read through the draft she was unhappy with how passive a character he became. On her blog, Meyer wrote about how she fixed this plot problem: "So I decided to do away with the amnesia entirely, which changed the basis of a lot of scenes throughout the book. Chapters and chapters had been dedicated to Scarlet and Wolf trying to find out more about his past—hunting down police records and the like—and those chapters now either had to be deleted or altered to fit with Wolf's new reality."

Meyer reviews her list of major issues and begins thinking about how to fix them. She goes through her manuscript chapter by chapter and begins to rewrite, makes edits and otherwise revises the story.

STEP 6: REVISIONS

After Meyer gets her second draft in order she focuses on rereading her manuscript several more times. Each time she's looking for things she doesn't like or places where a scene or a plot line could be strengthened. She continues to take notes and continues to read and reread her manuscript until she is happy with the overall story and her writing.

STEP 7: BETA READERS AND FINAL REVISIONS

Meyer shares her manuscript with beta readers—a group of four people (three readers plus her editor)—who read her manuscript and provide feedback on plot points in the story that don't work well, when the pacing of the book slows down, when suspense falls flat, when details don't make sense, or if places in the story need further clarification. Some of her betas are also great with grammar and punctuation and focus more on the structure of her writing than the story itself. Once she gathers this feedback, she

Editing and rewriting are major parts of the writing process. Marissa Meyer worked with her editors, as well as her own team of beta readers, to refine each novel.

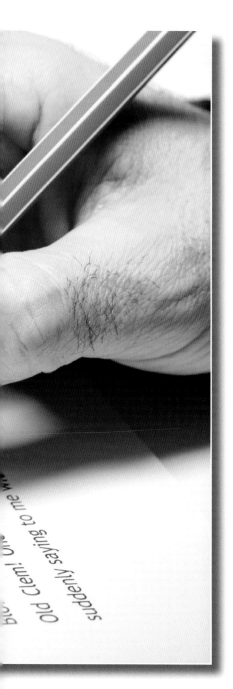

reviews their comments, thinks about their suggestions and implements the changes she thinks will strengthen the story. She then completes a final revision of the manuscript.

STEP 8: TWEAKING AND POLISHING

Meyer completes a final set of tweaking and polishing to her story. She reviews the manuscript for clutch phrases, or default phrases or descriptors writers tend to use repeatedly; to make her writing as tight as possible; and to complete one final read-through to make sure she has caught everything she hopes to. The manuscript is then sent to her editor.

STEP 9: THE PUBLISHER'S EDITORIAL PROCESS

This final step in her process is Meyer's last review of her manuscript after it has been copyedited and typeset by her publishing house's editorial and production teams. This happens once she receives the book laid out in the way a reader will see it when it's in book form. In this new format, Meyer sometimes finds things she didn't catch in her previous rounds of editing.

GETTING PUBLISHED

Without realizing that fairy tales would soon enjoy a resurgence, Meyer unknowingly tapped into the next big trend in publishing and entertainment when she began pitching *Cinder* to literary agents for representation in 2010.

TAPPING INTO THE FAIRY TALE CRAZE

Like all genres of entertainment, trends are cyclical in the publishing world. Since 2005, with the breakout success of *The Twilight Saga* by Stephanie Meyers, numerous televisions shows, such as *The Vampire Diaries,* vampire-themed books, and movies have dominated reading lists and viewership. As the interest in vampires began to die down, fairy tales started to gain momentum as the next genre of choice. TV shows, such as ABC's *Once Upon a Time* and NBC's *Grimm*, both of which feature popular characters from classic and contemporary fairy tales, grew in popularity. A number of movies—*Snow White and the Huntsman*, *Mirror, Mirror*, and *Disney's Cinderella*—have all been hits at the box office.

Meyer told The Book Wars, a blog written by a group of graduates from the children's literature program at the University of British Columbia, that she attributes the current interest in fairy tales to relatbility. "I think the reason for their popularity comes more from the inherent themes in the stories and how they relate to our basic human needs

In recent years, fantasy television shows like *Grimm* and *Once Upon a Time* drew large audiences. The cast of *Grimm*—shown here at Comic-Con International 2015—became international stars because of the show's popularity.

and desires. Cinderella is an excellent example. The archetypal 'rags to riches' tale is something every person understands and can relate to—we all want to improve our standing in society, we all want to believe that by working hard we can achieve happiness and comfort."

CRAFTING THE LUNAR CHRONICLES SERIES

As Meyer worked on her draft of *Cinder*, she kept thinking about the two other drafts she wrote during NaNoWriMo. Soon she found herself plotting a four-book series with lead characters based on some of her favorite fairy tales.

The Lunar Chronicles came about after Meyer developed a list of her ten favorite fairy tales. She spent time brainstorming different ways to tell each story with a science-fiction spin. While she was writing *Cinder* she was developing plot ideas for the next three books in the series: *Scarlet*, *Cress* and *Winter*. All four books in the Lunar Chronicles series build on the initial plot of *Cinder*, with new characters introduced in each successive novel.

The Lunar Chronicles has one continuous story line. Cinder is the main character throughout the series, but in each book she meets other characters that she joins forces with against an evil queen. In

WHY IS *CINDER* SET IN CHINA?

"Ye Xian" is a Chinese fairy tale that is similar in its plot to *Cinderella*. "Ye Xian" is one of the oldest known versions of *Cinderella* and was first published in the ninth century compilation *Miscellaneous Morsels from Youyang*. Because of this rich history, Meyer purposely decided to set her futuristic version of *Cinderella* in New Beijing. On her website, she explains: "Some scholars believe that the earliest Cinderella tale came from ninth century China. Additionally, some believe that the iconic glass slipper (which was gold in the Grimm version) came to us from China's tradition of foot-binding and a culture in which women were praised for tiny feet. So having *Cinder* set in China was my way of paying homage to the story's roots." Meyer also has a personal connection to the Asian country. She spent ten days in China as a child and as a result she developed a fascination with the country and its culture.

an interview with TeenReads.com, Meyer said: "It was my plan fairly early on to have all four books in the series add up to one continuous story, and as I brainstormed the plot, it became clear that the story was going to revolve around two main characters: Cinder and evil Queen Levana. But part of the fun

The tale of Little Red Riding Hood's encounter with the wolf has been a folklore favorite for centuries before Meyer used the basic idea for *Scarlet*. The first official version was actually penned in 1697 by French author Charles Perrault.

for me is mixing all of the fairy tales together and having these characters cross paths with each other as they move in and out of their own stories. As the story goes on, we get to see how Cinderella's prince might react to the Big Bad Wolf or how Rapunzel might get along with Snow White's hunter."

While each book is based on a different fairy tale, Cinder continues to be the main protagonist throughout the four books and is the main star of the entire series. In an interview with *Publishers Weekly*, Meyer described how all four of the Lunar Chronicles' stories intersect: "The story splits off and starts following new heroines until all the paths intertwine, and they must join forces to fight their common enemy, the Lunar Queen."

The Lunar Chronicles begins with *Cinder*, which is based on *Cinderella*. Meyer offers a synopsis on her website:

> Cinder, a gifted mechanic, is a cyborg. She's a second-class citizen with a mysterious past, reviled by her stepmother and blamed for her stepsister's illness. But when her life becomes intertwined with the handsome Prince Kai's, she suddenly finds herself at the center of an intergalactic struggle, and a forbidden attraction. Caught between duty and freedom, loyalty and betrayal, she must uncover secrets about her past in order to protect her world's future.

In *Scarlet*, based on *Little Red Riding Hood*, Cinder crosses paths with Scarlet and Wolf while unraveling a mystery. A synopsis on Meyer's website reads:

> Halfway around the world, Scarlet Benoit's grandmother is missing. It turns out there are many things Scarlet doesn't know about her grandmother and the grave danger she has lived in her whole life. When Scarlet encounters Wolf, a street fighter who may have information as to her grandmother's

Marissa Meyer's futuristic city of New Beijing, China, is based on the actual city of Beijing, China. Its modernist architecture and space-age feel provided Meyer with the perfect inspiration for her sci-fi novel.

whereabouts, she has no choice but to trust him, though he clearly has a few dark secrets of his own. Together with Cinder, Scarlet and Wolf must stay one step ahead of the vicious Lunar Queen who will do anything to make Prince Kai her husband, her king, her prisoner.

Meyer set *Scarlet* in France, where there is a rich history of werewolf folklore and mythology. She told TeenReads.com: "I saw a TV documentary about 'The Beast of Gévaudan,' which was a creature that supposedly roamed the French countryside in the 18th century. There was a slew of killings in a few rural towns and the townspeople attributed it to this beast, which they believed was a werewolf. This legend was also

igure de la Bête feroce ne
r arrache les mamelles bu

ne qui devore les Hommes et principalement les Femmes et les
le cœur et le foye et leur arrache la tete. Elle fait ce carn

No stranger to using historical texts as inspiration, Meyer used the legendary "beast of Gévaudan" as a source for her werewolf mythology in *Scarlet*. This engraving shows one of the old depictions of the creature from centuries ago.

53

where the idea of werewolves being vulnerable to silver bullets comes from. So that old tale of were-wolves, murders and terror inspired the rural French setting for *Scarlet*."

The third book in the series, *Cress*, is based on *Rapunzel*. But Meyer's twist on the fairy tale has Cress is stuck in a satellite orbiting Earth instead of hidden away in a tower. Cress also happens to be a skilled computer hacker who is forced to work for Queen Levana. Meyer offers this summary on her website:

When a daring rescue goes awry, the group is splintered. Cress finally has her freedom, but it comes at a higher price than she'd ever expected. Meanwhile, Queen Levana will let nothing prevent her marriage to Emperor Kai, especially the cyborg mechanic. Cress, Scarlet and Cinder may not have signed up to save the world, but they may be the only hope the world has.

The final book of the Lunar Chronicles, *Winter,* is based on *Snow White and the Seven Dwarfs*, and completes the series. A summary of *Winter* introduces Princess Winter, the stepdaughter of Queen Levana:

Princess Winter is admired by the Lunar people for her grace and kindness, and despite the scars that mar her face, her beauty is said to be even more breathtaking than that of her stepmother, Queen Levana. Winter despises her stepmother, and knows Levana won't approve of her feelings for her childhood friend—the handsome palace guard, Jacin. But Winter isn't as weak as Levana believes her to be and she's been undermining her stepmother's wishes for years. Together with the cyborg mechanic, Cinder, and her allies, Winter might even have the power to launch a revolution and win a war that's been raging for far too long.

Winter, at 824 pages, is the longest book in the Lunar Chronicles series.

PITCHING THE SERIES TO AN AGENT

Once Meyer completed a solid draft of *Cinder* she began drafting query letters to agents to find someone to represent her to publishing houses. Meyer's query letter included a complete draft of *Cinder*, the first 50 pages of *Scarlet* and summaries of *Cress* and *Winter*. Her goal was to hook an agent on the

Jill Grinberg of Jill Grinberg Literary Management represents Scott Westerfeld, the author of *The Leviathan Trilogy* and one of Marissa Meyer's role models. The same agency first signed Meyer herself.

appeal of the entire series, not just the first book. Meyer knew pitching a four-book series by an author who had never been published before was a big risk, but it paid off.

Meyer began querying or contacting agents on August 16, 2010. Within two months she had three offers for representation. Meyer signed with Jill Grinberg of Jill Grinberg Literary Management, who happened to be the first agent she queried. Among the best-selling authors Grinberg represents is Scott Westerfeld, the author of *The Leviathan Trilogy* and one of Meyer's role models.

HOW TO FIND AN AGENT

If you are an aspiring author, finding an agent is an important step in the publishing process. An agent will identify the best publishing houses that are most likely to be interested in your manuscript. They not only represent you and your book to publishers, but they also provide you with valuable feedback on your manuscript so it is in prime condition when it is presented to editors. They negotiate contracts if your book sells, explain the details of contracts and negotiate terms, such as advancements and royalties. They will also help you identify future publishing opportunities. Finding the right agent is important. Not all agents represent all types of writers. Some agents are interested only in young adult or children's literature. Some prefer science fiction, fantasy or paranormal. Others are interested in romance, women's fiction or nonfiction. You'll want to identify an agent that specializes in your genre of writing.

When you are ready to begin contacting an agent with a query letter, you should compile a list of agents that represent the genre of your book and tailor your letter and materials specifically to each one. Agents have specific guidelines on their websites for what they like to see in a query letter.

Grinberg offered some minor suggestions to Meyer on her manuscript for *Cinder* and once it was ready they began submitting it to publishers. "Jill and I worked on our submission package for two weeks, during which time I wrote 50 pages of book two and detailed synopses of books three and four. We sent everything out on a Friday and had our first offer on Monday."

Meyer experienced an unusually fast submission process. On Friday, October 29, 2010, Meyer and Grinberg began submitting the manuscript to publishers. By the following Monday, November 1, 2010, which happened to be the two year anniversary from the day she began writing *Cinder*, Meyer and Grinberg had an offer. A week later, the series went to auction between two publishing houses. When a book or series goes "to auction" it means more than one publishing house is interested in buying the manuscript and they are making different offers to an agent. Meyer accepted an offer from Macmillan's Feiwel and Friends on November 11, 2010, in the amount of $800,000, as an advance on the entire four-book series. Jean Feiwel, vice president and publisher of Feiwel and Friends, is behind numerous blockbuster book series, including *The Baby-Sitters Club*, *Goosebumps*, and *The Magic School Bus*. When Feiwel was the senor vice president and publisher of Scholastic Trade Books she was the

Jean Feiwel *(seated, left)* has helped publish a number of best-selling novels, including *The Baby-Sitters Club*, by author Ann Martin *(right)*, *Goosebumps*, and the American editions of the *Harry Potter* series.

American publisher of the *Harry Potter* series.

In an interview with *Publishers Weekly*, Jean Feiwel said the *Cinder* manuscript arrived just as the excitement over *The Hunger Games*, a science-fiction series by Suzanne Collins, was beginning to wane. The *Cinder* manuscript caught the attention of nearly everyone on her staff. "Everyone who read it loved it, including publicity, sales, and marketing people," she told the publication. "Over the two-day auction, people kept coming into my office to say, 'Make *sure* you get this book.' There would have been a lot of disappointed people if I hadn't managed to acquire it."

FOUR

CHAPTER

A BEST-SELLING SERIES HITS THE SHELVES

*C*inder became an instant best seller due in large part to a multimedia marketing campaign aimed at teen readers. With a full-fledged marketing rollout that included social media, a press tour for Meyer, articles in national newspapers and a high-end, Hollywood-style book trailer, *Cinder* debuted on the *New York Times* best-seller list.

A BIG DEBUT

Following an extensive Facebook campaign; promotion on Tor.com, an online science fiction magazine with a monthly readership of 1.5 million; a pre-publication excerpt in *USA Today* and a big-budget, Hollywood-style book trailer, *Cinder* was released on January 3, 2012, and in its first week it debuted on the *New York Times* best-seller list.

Critical response to *Cinder* was good, which helped to boost sales. The *Los Angeles Times* called the book "refreshing" and praised the character of Cinder. *Publishers Weekly* positively reviewed the book, saying that the characters are "easy to get invested in." *Booklist* called *Cinder* a "fresh spin on 'Cinderella.'" *The Wall Street Journal* wrote that the book was an "undemanding and surprisingly good-natured read." *Kidzworld* stated that *Cinder* was "an amazing story about love that comes in mysterious packages."

For some books, positive critical reviews don't always align with an increase in book sales. Sometimes a critic loves a book but the story just doesn't connect with its audience. The opposite can also be true. An audience ends up loving a book that critics find to be poorly written or with a plot that isn't soundly constructed.

Scarlet, the second novel in the Lunar Chronicles series, was released on February 5, 2013. It debuted at #4 on the *New York Times* best-seller list. *Scarlet* is based on *Little Red Riding Hood* and as Meyer was developing the book she wanted to choose a fairy tale that was well known but that gave her some room for re-invention. She told TeenReads. com that as she brainstormed ideas for which fairy

Social media has changed publishing. With Facebook buzz, tweets on Twitter, and Instagram posts, authors can connect directly with fans and more easily market and sell their books as well.

tale she wanted to use for her second novel, *"Little Red Riding Hood* kept popping to the surface. I knew it was familiar enough that readers would have an instant connection to it, while also having a lot of wiggle room for me to re-envision the story in my futuristic, high-tech world. I was particularly excited to see what could be done with the character of the Big Bad Wolf."

The third novel in the series, *Cress,* was released on January 4, 2014, and is based on *Rapunzel*. Like in her previous novels, Meyer has kept several of the iconic pieces of the fairy tale in her retelling while making the story her own. "You still have the tower symbolism and this witch who's keeping her there. Rapunzel still has long, flowing locks of hair. Those iconic moments are still there, but then it does take on a life of its own in the world as she meets up with Cinder and Scarlet and the other characters," Meyer told *USA Today* in an interview prior to the release of the book.

The fourth and final novel in the Lunar Chronicles series is *Winter,* which is based on *Snow White and the Seven Dwarfs* and was released on November 10, 2015. Winter is the evil queen's stepdaughter and has witnessed how her stepmother's lunar powers have turned the woman into a tyrant. As a result, Winter decides that she will never use her pow-ers. But, as Winter quickly learns, when a Lunar decides not to use his or her powers it slowly starts to drive them mad and Winter finds her mental state slowly deteriorating.

Into the Woods, a popular musical turned feature film, has combined numerous fairy tales into one imaginative story. This still is from the musical's production at the Châtelet Theatre in Paris and depicts the tale of *Rapunzel*.

With her novels based on popular fairy tales, Marissa Meyer tapped into an instant following of fans connected to a story they were already familiar with. The character of Snow White, for example, was instantly recognizable to readers.

Overall the series has remained popular since its launch. While Amazon updates their sales rankings hourly, on the afternoon of May 6, 2015, for example, *Cinder*, *Scarlet* and *Cress* were among the top six in sales in the Teen & Young Adult Fairy Tales & Folklore Adaptation category.

CRAFTING STRONG CHARACTERS AND CREATING POWERFUL STORYLINES

Meyer was adamant about one thing as she wrote her novels: the characters, while flawed, should be strong and courageous, especially the women in her stories. In an interview with TeenReads.com, Meyer talked about why she wanted to move away from the classic way in which fairy tales portray women as in need of being saved or otherwise helped in some way by a male character. "I didn't want to rely on the stereotypes of popular fairy tale characters, and so I try to avoid them wherever possible. That started with Cinderella—Cinder isn't a pushover and Prince Kai isn't a dandy. For me, it wouldn't be any fun to write about those characters. I like heroes who are courageous, who stand up for what they believe in and who take steps to right the injustices they see."

WHO'S WHO IN THE LUNAR CHRONICLES

- Linh Cinder – a cyborg living with her stepmother and her two stepsisters, who works as a mechanic in a booth at a marketplace where she meets Prince Kai, who requests her to fix his personal android.
- Scarlet Benoit – the granddaughter of Michelle Benoit, a farmer and former military pilot who has suddenly gone missing. On Scarlet's journey to find her grandmother, she teams up with a street fighter named Wolf and learns from him that her *grandmére* may be hiding secrets regarding Princess Selene, the lunar princess.
- Crescent Moon "Cress" Darnel – a banished hacker who is somehow caught up in Cinder and her crew's plot to overthrow the wicked Lunar queen.
- Winter – Queen Levana's stepdaughter. She has lived on Luna in the palace but grown up with her stepmother and seen how, when Levana uses her lunar powers, it's turned her into a heartless tyrant. Winter has decided never to use her lunar gift, so she has not used her Lunar glamour since she was twelve.
- Queen Levana – the Lunar Queen, who uses her gift of extremely powerful glamour to brainwash people to do as she tells them.

- Prince Kai – the crown prince of the Eastern Commonwealth until his father, Emperor Rikan, passes away. Kai becomes the commonwealth's new emperor.
- Ze'ev "Z" Kesley – also known as Wolf, is a former special operative in the Lunar army and becomes Scarlet's protector.
- Jacin – formerly one of the palace guards of the Lunar royal family. He grew up with Winter and they became best friends.
- Iko – an android that belonged to the Linh family and a friend of Cinder's.

With four novels all set in the same world and all intimately connected with interwoven plotlines and characters, Meyer told BiblioFriend. com that weaving the stories together was a huge undertaking. "The biggest challenge of the series was balancing the multiple plotlines, and making sure that the reader feels invested in all plotlines, and they care about every plotline, without making it feel too lopsided or heavy," she told the website. This balance took planning and Meyer even needed to reread her previous novels as she began writing *Cress* and *Winter* to make sure plot points stayed cohesive, characters remained consistent and the story didn't leave any gaping holes for the reader.

CONNECTING WITH FANS

Fan reaction to the Lunar Chronicles has been intense. Meyer has attended Comic-Con International: San Diego, one of the largest show-cases in the world of comic books and science fiction/fantasy-related film, television, books and other entertainment. At Comic-Con, Meyer has participated on panel discussions on topics such as remixing fairy tales and when tough female characters fall in love.

There are several hundred pieces of fan fiction set in the world of the Lunar Chronicles, which Meyer appreciates given her history writing *Sailor Moon* fan fiction. She told fanbolt.com: "I am totally an advocate for fan fiction. I love it. It's fans being out there, being so excited about your work, and those are the people who are going to spread the word of mouth and the people that are going to turn the fandom into something that hangs around for a while. I think that if someone can take an idea, something that started out as fan fiction, and then turn it around into something that's uniquely their own

Fans often enage in cosplay as popular sci-fi characters, like this fan dressed as Chibiusa from *Sailor Moon* at Comic-Con International in San Diego, California. Meyer even holds fan art and costume contests via her website.

and able to become published, I think that's fantastic!"

Fan art has become another venue in which Meyer's fans have expressed their love and admiration for Meyer and the characters of the Lunar Chronicles. "I love seeing fanart! It's been one of the greatest honors to know that readers have been inspired to create something of their own, and I really enjoy seeing how readers interpret what the characters look like or how some scenes might have played out differently. That tells me that readers want to continue to spend time in the world of the Lunar Chronicles, and there's no greater compliment than that," Meyer told TeenReads.com.

Meyer's publisher has created numerous fan art contests in which fans can enter original artwork, and don costumes based on the various characters in her work, and from the fairy tale universe in general. Contests have included opportunities for fans to submit illustrations that depict the Lunar insignia for Queen Levana using her mystical mirror, artwork for sticker contests and a fan video contest that asks fans to describe why they love the Lunar Chronicles and to tell Meyer and her publisher who their favorite character is and why they love him or her.

THE LUNAR CHRONICLES ON THE BIG SCREEN

The movie rights to the Lunar Chronicles have been optioned by a film studio and a screenplay is currently in development. In the film industry, an option refers to an agreement between the author of a book and a movie studio, a production company or a producer that is interested in developing a book into a film or television project. A studio, production company or producer obtains the right to buy the rights to a book before a particular date. An option doesn't necessarily mean a movie or television series will be produced. It often means a studio or producer will begin to develop the project to see if it becomes viable by an agreed upon date. If a project doesn't come to fruition, the option rights expire and the author can pursue other optioning agreements.

In an interview with Bibliofiend.com, Meyer spoke about her hopes for how a studio would approach film adaptations of her books. "I would hope they would stay true to the characters. I understand that they may not always be aiming at the same audience, or certain plot or world-building things that they can do better or can't do as well in a movie format versus a book format. But I would really hope they would keep the essence of the characters."

The studio that optioned the rights to the Lunar Chronicles has not been publically announced.

The Lunar Chronicles series is available in nearly thirty countries around the world, including Australia, South America, and throughout Europe and Asia. It has also been translated into more than twenty-five different langauges.

PROJECTS IN DEVELOPMENT

Since the success of the Lunar Chronicles, Meyer has begun to branch out in her writing. She has published numerous short stories and several companion novels, all set in the world of the Lunar Chronicles. In 2013, Meyer's publisher, Feiwel and Friends, offered Meyer a two-book deal in which one of the books will feature the backstory of the Queen of Hearts from *Alice in Wonderland*. Meyer is also in the early stages of researching and developing a new series that will be based on her interest in superheroes.

SHORT STORIES

Meyer has written several short stories that take place within the world of The Lunar

Marissa Meyer is developing future projects, including stories centered around the Queen of Hearts, the main villain in Lewis Carroll's 1865 book, *Alice in Wonderland*. This is an illustration of the Queen of Hearts by John Tenniel.

Chronicles. These stories are available on Wattpad (http://www.wattpad.com), a social community for readers and writers who are interested in sharing their work with others. Authors publish work, original or fan fiction, to the Wattpad website and readers can opt to follow authors, which means the site will notify a reader when a favorite writer has posted new work. The site is free to join and only requires members to register with a log in and password.

The short stories that take place within the world of the Lunar Chronicles are either prequels, where their events happened before a certain novel in the Lunar Chronicles series, or they share the same setting but include characters that are different from those in the main series.

In *Cinder*, Linh Cinder's stepmother blames her for Letumosis, a disease that causes a plague in the years before *Cinder* is set. It's also the illness Cinder's stepsister suffers from. *Glitches,* which was released on January 18, 2012, is a prequel to *Cinder.* A prequel is an early part of a story that takes place before the plot of a main story. *Glitches* lets readers see the results of the plague, which later plays out in *Cinder*. Readers witness the emotional toll the plague takes on Linh Cinder, an event that may or may not have been a glitch, or malfunction, in the Lunar Chronicles world. *Glitches* has more than 37,000 reads on Wattpad.

In *The Queen's Army,* a prequel to *Scarlet,* readers are introduced to the method the Queen uses to recruit soldiers into her army and how one young boy will do anything to avoid becoming the monster Queen Levana wants him to be. *The Queen's Army* was released on November 20, 2012, on Wattpad and has more than 90,000 reads.

The Little Android, a retelling of Hans Christian Andersen's "The Little Mermaid," is set in the world of the Lunar Chronicles. Released on January 27, 2014, the story centers on Mech6.0, an android that saves the life of a hardware engineer and somehow falls in love with him, even though androids aren't meant to be able to develop emotions, reasoning or feelings of love. Available on Wattpad, *The Little Android* has more than 587,000 reads.

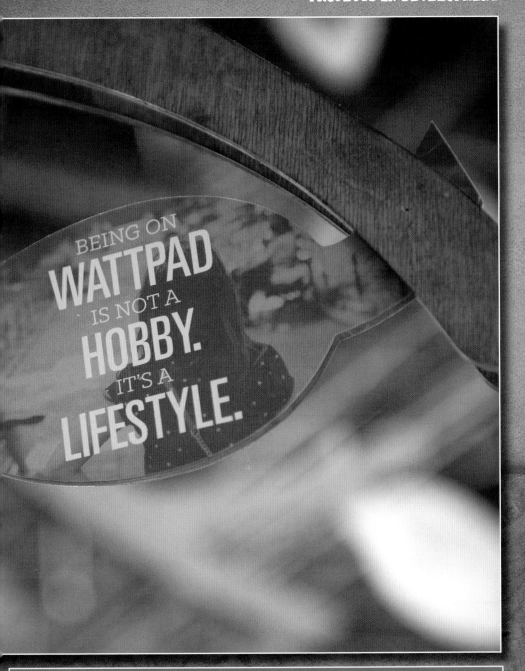

BEING ON WATTPAD IS NOT A HOBBY. IT'S A LIFESTYLE.

Several projects of Meyer's have appeared on Wattpad, an online writing community, where her fans can read stories set in, or related to, the Lunar Chronicles.

Carswell's Guide to Being Lucky is based on the life of thirteen-year-old Carswell Thorne. Carswell has big plans involving a spaceship and a one-way trip to escape Los Angeles. Fans who subscribe to Meyer's newsletter via her website are emailed this short story. Carswell later appears in the Lunar Chronicles and becomes a love interest for Cress.

A COMPANION NOVEL TO THE LUNAR CHRONICLES

Released in January 2015, *Fairest: Levana's Story* is a prequel that focuses on the origin of Queen Levana, the main antagonist of the Lunar Chronicles. The story begins when Levana is fifteen years old and covers roughly ten years of Levana's life, up until about a decade before the beginning of *Cinder*.

Meyer originally wrote *Fairest* after she kept hitting roadblocks in the plotting of *Winter*. She kept thinking about the motivation of Queen Levana. In an interview with *Deseret News* Meyer said, "I've always wondered what could make a woman so vain and so crazy that she would kill her stepdaughter just so that she could remain the most beautiful in the kingdom." When she couldn't fit the Queen's backstory into *Winter*, and after her attempts to work through a particularly difficult portion of *Winter's* manuscript, Meyer took a break. In a week she wrote *Fairest*. "It was the fastest story I've ever written," Meyer told *Deseret News*.

When Meyer wrote *Fairest* she envisioned the story as a companion piece to *Winter*, an extra story after the main novel ends or as a promotional e-book similar to other short stories she produced, such as *Glitches* or *The Queen's Army*. When her publishers read the novel, they had other ideas. After reading *Fairest* they were convinced Meyer's fans needed to understand Queen Levana's back-story before the release of *Winter*. So they published the book as a stand-alone novel. For Meyer, *Fairest* is a fun piece of writing that allowed her to explore a background story she couldn't fit in to the Lunar Chronicles world. "As writers, we have so many ideas in the back of our head about these little stories that happen to our characters and little things in the world that happen that we don't get to share in the books," Meyer told *Deseret News*. "It's always fun to take a few days and explore different aspects."

NEW STORIES

In 2013, with a new two-book deal from Feiwel and Friends, Meyer began to develop *Heartless*, which was released in the fall of 2015. *Heartless* features the Queen of Hearts from *Alice in Wonderland*.

The idea for *Heartless* came about from a conversation between Meyer and one of her agents. On her blog, Meyer wrote, "I absolutely loved *Wicked* by Gregory Maguire—both the book and the musical. A few years ago, right after *Cinder* sold, I was having lunch with my agent and talking about fairy tale retellings. I brought up *Wicked* and *Confessions of an Ugly Stepsister* and mentioned that I thought it would be awesome if Mr. Maguire told the story of the Queen of Hearts. My foreign rights agent—smart cookie that she is—said, 'Well, why don't *you* write it?'"

Heartless will be a standalone novel and not part of a new series. However, on her blog, Meyer wrote that while she is keeping an open mind for a second novel set in the world of *Heartless*, the second book of her publishing deal will most likely kick off a new series.

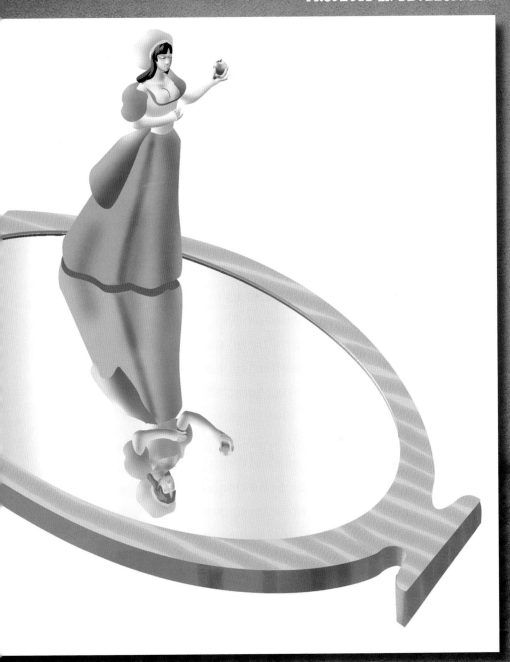

Marissa Meyer is exploring other writing projects that center on side characters in other fairy tales. With a wide variety of old stories and her own new universes to draw on, the possibilites for future projects are endless.

PROJECTS BUBBLING ON THE BACK BURNER

In numerous interviews, Meyer has spoken about her interest in writing a series that could feature superheroes. On her blog she announced that she has begun researching and developing a series she has tentatively titled *The Gatlon Trilogy*. Meyer has offered a summary of her initial idea for the series:

> There are two rival schools in Gatlon City: the respected and exclusive Morris Academy, which has turned many an evolved youth into celebrity superheroes, and the Gatlon School for the Gifted, which has a slightly less impressive reputation. Students of Gatlon tend to be relegated to minions, placeholders, or—at best—sidekicks. Clara has no interest in being a hero, but she does need answers. Her invisible, mischievous pet Thunderbird, Tondra, is dying, and she refuses to let him go without a fight. Unfortunately, there seems to be a lot more happening in Gatlon than just a sickly mythical bird. Crime is on the rise, the police have gone complacent, and a new team of vigilantes is causing more problems than they're fixing. When Clara and her peers find themselves swept up in the chaos and

no longer able to tell the good guys from the bad, no one is sure which side of hero vs. villain they'll fall on.

MEYER MEDIA

Like almost any other writer who is building a fan base in the current social media landscape, Meyer makes sure she engages with fans and generates buzz and excitement for her new projects.

Her website, http://www.marissameyer.com, is a one-stop shop for news about her books, her personal blog, as well as links to her publishers, a calendar of events (including appearances and signings, whether at bookstores, libraries, or conventions), and more.

It also provides links to other faces of Meyer online, including her Twitter account (@marissa_meyer), a tool that few authors for young people do without these days.

There are still other ways to connect with and follow her progress, including her Facebook fan page account (https://www.facebook.com/MarissaMeyerAuthor), her profile page on Goodreads, the literary social network, as well as interviews on sites like Teenreads.com. Wherever fans choose to connect, a lively engagement with them is a part of the life of a modern writer.

A FUTURE OF BALANCING FAMILY LIFE AND WRITING

Meyer has had to adjust her writing schedule to accommodate her two young foster children, and has said in interviews that the pace at which she was writing may have to slow down so she can focus on raising her children. However, with numerous story ideas in development, she has no plans to stop writing. She also said in an interview with *The Phoenix New Times* that she has no plans to write outside of the science fiction, fantasy and young-adult genres. Fueled by her own interest in the genre and her growing fan base of both teen and adult readers, Meyer plans to further develop projects aimed at her young adult audience with the hopes that her adult fans will follow her as she introduces new worlds and new characters. "YA [young adult] is pushing the boundaries," Meyer told *The Phoenix New Times*. "Many studies have shown that a majority of young-adult readers are adults, so I think the numbers speak for themselves."

ON MARISSA MEYER

Birth date: February 19, 1984

Birthplace: Tacoma, Washington

Current residence: Tacoma, Washington

First publication: *Cinder* (The Lunar Chronicles, book one)

Marital status: Married to Jesse Taylor

Family: Two foster children

Education: Bachelor of Arts, Creative Writing, Pacific Lutheran University; Master of Arts, Publishing, Pace University

Favorite book: *Pride and Prejudice* by Jane Austen

Awards: Amazon Children's Choice Book Award for *Cinder*; Amazon Children's Choice Book Award for *Cress*; 2012 Goodreads Choice Awards nominee for *Cinder*.

ON MARISSA MEYER'S WORK

The Lunar Chronicles

January 2012: *Cinder* (The Lunar Chronicles, book one); Amazon Children's Choice Book Award

February 2013: *Scarlet* (The Lunar Chronicles, book two)

February 2014: *Cress* (The Lunar Chronicles, book three); Amazon Children's Choice Book Award

November 2015: *Winter* (The Lunar Chronicles, book four)

The Lunar Chronicles Companion Stories

January 2015: *Fairest: The Lunar Chronicles: Levana's Story*

*Glitches** (prequel to *Cinder*)

*The Queen's Army** (prequel to *Scarlet*)

Carswell's Guide to Being Lucky†

Non-series Books

February 2016: *Heartless*

Non-series Short Stories
"The Little Android"*

* Only available on Meyer's Wattpad page.
† Only available by subscribing to Meyer's
    newsletter.

Cinder (The Lunar Chronicles, book one)

"Author Marissa Meyer rocks the fractured fairy tale genre with a sci-fi twist on Cinderella."—*The Seattle Times*

"First in the Lunar Chronicles series, this futuristic twist on Cinderella retains just enough of the original that readers will enjoy spotting the subtle similarities. But debut author Meyer's brilliance is in sending the story into an entirely new, utterly thrilling dimension."—*Publishers Weekly*

"This series opener and debut offers a high coolness factor by rewriting Cinderella as a kickass mechanic in a plague-ridden future."—*Kirkus Reviews*

"Fairy tales are becoming all the rage, with the TV shows *Once Upon a Time* and *Grimm* spinning them through a modern filter. The 26-year-old Meyer's debut novel *Cinder*, though, combines a classic folk tale with hints of *The Terminator* and *Star Wars* in the first book of *The Lunar Chronicles* young-adult series due out Jan. 3."—*USAToday.com*

"Singing mice and glass slippers are replaced with snarky androids and mechanical feet in this richly imagined and darkly subversive retelling of 'Cinderella.'"—*BCCB*

"What they [readers] do not know until they begin
turning the pages of this fable-turned-dystopian-
science-fiction novel, is that Meyer's
embellishments create a spellbinding story of their
own."—*VOYA*

"*Cinder* is loads of fun—mostly due to seeing a
familiar story play out in a new setting, but
Cinder herself is also a tough, smart, mouthy,
resourceful heroine, so spending almost 400
pages with her is completely enjoyable—and
I'm totally, totally looking forward to the next one
in the series." —*Bookshelves of Doom*

Scarlet (The Lunar Chronicles, book two)
"It's another Marissa Meyer roller coaster ride, part
science fiction/fantasy, part political machina-
tion with a hint of romance. Readers will be
pushed into a horrific alternate universe where
violence, especially mind manipulation and
control, create ethical and life-threatening
situations for both teens. With at least one
more Lunar Chronicle to come, the suspense
continues. And which fairy tale will Meyer
morph next?"—*Booklist*, starred review

"Returning fans of Meyer's *Cinder* will gladly sink their
teeth into this ambitious, wholly satisfying
sequel."—*Publishers Weekly*

"The author has stepped up the intrigue and plot from the first novel, and readers will be eagerly awaiting the next."—*School Library Journal*

"Further development of this futuristic world plus plenty of action, surprises, and a fast pace will keep readers invested in their journey." —*The Horn Book*

"The sci-fi elements are stronger than the fairy-tale allusions this time out, but the story remains just as absorbing . . . Readers will be thrilled to discover that this steampunky fairy-tale/sci-fi mash-up promises two more installments."—*BCCB*

Cress (The Lunar Chronicles, book three)
"Meyer continues to show off her storytelling prowess, keeping readers engaged in a wide cast of characters while unfolding a layered plot that involves warring governments and a fast-spreading plague. The momentum Meyer built in the first two books continues to accelerate as the stakes grow higher for Cinder and her friends. The next installment cannot come fast enough."—*Publishers Weekly*

"Once again, Meyer offers up a science fiction fantasy page-turner that salutes women's intelligence and empowerment. . . . Old and new romances, unfinished story lines, and the prognostication of wartime horrors all pave the way for Meyer's much anticipated next install-ment, *Winter*, expected in 2015." —*Booklist*

Fairest: The Lunar Chronicles: Levana's Story

"She loves fiercely and kills with little remorse; her iron grip over the Lunar people is equal parts impressive and terrifying. Queen Levana from 'The Lunar Chronicles' is more than a beautiful villain. In this prequel, Meyer explains how she went from lonely, shy second daughter to the most feared and relentless woman in the uni-verse." —*School Library Journal*

"Meyers seamlessly builds and weaves twists and jabs into Levana's story. Sheltered, lonely, and desperate is a dangerous mix for someone who is rising into power. *Fairest* explains how Levana came to be such a twisted, brutal character... Fans of the Lunar Chronicles must read *Fairest*."—YAbookscentral.com

February 19, 1984 Marissa Meyer is born.

May 2007 Meyer graduates from Pacific Lutheran University.

November 1, 2008 Meyer begins writing *Cinder* during National Novel Writing Month.

August 16, 2010 Meyer begins querying agents with her manuscript for *Cinder*.

October 29, 2010 Meyer and Jill Grinberg, her literary agent, began submitting the manuscript for *Cinder* to publishers

November 1, 2010 Meyer has her first offer from a publisher to buy *Cinder*.

November 11, 2010 Meyer accepts an offer to sell *Cinder* to Macmillan's Feiwel and Friends publishing house.

January 3, 2012 *Cinder* is published.

January 18, 2012 *Glitches* is released on Wattpad.

November 20, 2012 *The Queen's Army* is released on Wattpad.

February 5, 2013 *Scarlet* is published.

January 4, 2014 *Cress* is published.

January 27, 2014 *The Little Android* is released on Wattpad.

December 2014 Meyer and her husband become parents to two foster children.

January 27, 2015 *Fairest: Levana's Story* is published.

November 10, 2015 *Winter* is published.

ANTAGONIST The adversary or opponent in a story.

ARCHETYPAL An example that is perfect.

BETA A version of a product or story that is almost finished and is ready for testing.

BRAINSTORM A series of ideas.

CONFLICT A struggle for power or a disagreement between two parties.

DEBUT The first time something is revealed in public.

DEPICT To show or describe something.

DEPOSITORY A place where something can be kept safe or hidden.

FANTASY Fueled by the imagination or a setting in a made up world.

GENRE A particular category of literature, TV show, or film.

GRANDMÜRE A French word that means grandmother.

GRAPHIC ART Two-dimensional drawing or art that can include illustration, photography, writing, etc.

HEROINE The main female character of a story that exhibits courage and strength.

HISTORICAL DRAMA A story set in a particular time in history and based on real historical events or people.

ITERATION A new version or incarnation of a story.

KLINGON A member of a warlike human-alien species from the television series *Star Trek*.

MANUSCRIPT An original piece of writing before it is published.

MYSTICAL Having mystic or spiritual meaning.

ORIGINALITY New or different, not having been done before.

OUTLINE A preliminary, condensed view of a project or piece of writing.

PREQUEL An early part of a story that happens before the main plot of a novel or film.

PROMPT Quickly or on time.

PROOFREADER Someone who reads and corrects written work.

PROTAGONIST The hero or good guy of a story.

QUERY LETTER A letter written to an agent or publisher that outlines a piece of writing.

RELATABILITY Being able to relate to or understand.

RESURGENCE Growth or renewed interest after a period of no activity.

SCIENCE FICTION A genre of writing set in the future, often including advanced technology.

SOUNDTRACK Music that accompanies a film or TV show.

STEREOTYPE To believe something about an entire group of people.

TYPESETTER A person who sets type in an older style of publishing or printing.

VIRTUAL Existing on computers or on the Internet.

Canadian Children's Book Centre
Suite 217, 40 Orchard View Blvd.
Toronto, ON M4R 1B9
Website: http://www.bookcentre.ca
The Canadian Children's Book Centre is a not-for-
    profit organization that encourages, promotes
    and supports the reading, writing, illustrating,
    and publishing of Canadian books for young
    readers.

The Children's Literature Web Guide
University of Calgary
Calgary, Alberta, Canada
T2N 1N4
The Children's Literature Web Guide gathers together
    and categorizes the growing number of Internet
    resources related to books for children and
    young adults. The center also offers resources
    for writers, including an online book discussion
    group.

International Literacy Association
PO Box 8139
Newark, DE 19714-8139
Website: http://www.reading.org
As an advocate of excellence in teaching, ILA partici-
    pates actively in shaping sound public policy in
    literacy education.

The Kids Writing Club
Website: http://s4.zetaboards.com/KWC/index
The Kids Writing Club is a free, members only online
        writing club for kids to develop their writing
        abilities. Members can share their writing with
        other kids for feedback and advice.

Science Fiction and Fantasy Writers of America
SFWA, Inc.
PO Box 3238
Enfield, CT 06083-3238
Website: http://www.sfwa.org
A professional organization for authors of science
        fiction, fantasy, and related genres.

Society of Children's Book Writers and Illustrators
4727 Wilshire Blvd., Suite 301
Los Angeles, CA 90010
Website: http://www.scbwi.org
One of the largest existing organizations for writers
        and illustrators. It is the only professional organi-
        zation specifically for those individuals writing
        and illustrating for children and young adults in
        the fields of children's literature, magazines,
        film, television, and multimedia.

YA (Young Adult) Lit Chat
Website: http://yalitchat.com
A literary non-profit organization dedicated to foster-
        ing the advancement of young adult literature
        and the understanding of young adult culture

around the world, through the reading, writing, and publishing of young adult literature.

LIST OF WEBSITES

Because of the changing number of Internet links, Rosen Publishing has developed an online list of websites related to the subject of this book. This site is updated regularly. Please use this link to access the list:

http://www.rosenlinks.com/AAA/MMeyer

Aveyard, Victoria. *Red Queen*. New York, NY: Harper Teen, 2015.

Black, Holly. *The Darkest Part of the Forest*. New York, NY: Little, Brown Books for Your Readers, 2015.

Clare, Cassandra. *The Infernal Devices: Clockwork Angel (Book 1)*. New York, NY: Margaret K. McElderry Books, 2011.

Clare, Cassandra. *The Infernal Devices: Clockwork Princess (Book 3)*. New York, NY: Margaret K. McElderry Books, 2013.

Clare, Cassandra. *The Mortal Instruments: City of Ashes (Book 2)*. New York, NY: Margaret K. McElderry Books, 2009.

Clare, Cassandra. *The Mortal Instruments: City of Bones (Book 1)*. New York, NY: Margaret K. McElderry Books, 2008.

Collins, Suzanne. *The Hunger Games*. New York, NY: Scholastic Press, 2009.

Dashner, James. *The Maze Runner*. New York, NY: Random House/Delacorte Press, 2009.

Kaufman, Amie. *These Broken Stars*. New York, NY: Disney Hyperion, 2013

Landers, Melissa. *Alienated*. New York, NY: Disney Hyperion, 2014.

Roth, Veronica. *Allegiant*. New York, NY: Harper Collins/Katherine Tegen Books, 2013.

Sparkes, Kate. *Bound* (Bound Trilogy, Book One). Seattle, Washington: Amazon Digital Services, Inc./Sparrowcat Press, 2014.

Spooner, Meagan. *The Broken Stars.* New York, NY: Disney Hyperion, 2013.

Tolkien, J.R.R. *The Lord of the Rings.* New York, NY: Houghton Mifflin, 2012.

Weber, Mary. *Storm Siren.* New York, NY: HarperCollins Christian Publishing/Thomas Nelson, 2014.

Book Wars Blog. "Interview with Marissa Meyer."
September 3, 2013. Retrieved May 4, 2015
(https://thebookwars.wordpress.
com/2013/09/03/interview-with-marissa-meyer).

Cunningham, Joel. "8 Best-Sellers Started During
National Novel Writing Month." Barnesandnoble.
com, November 1, 2013. Retrieved April 17,
2015 (http://www.barnesandnoble.com/
blog/8-best-sellers-started-during-national-
novel-writing-month).

Ebook Friendly. "15 Most Popular Fan Fiction
Websites." Retrieved April 15, 2015 (http://
ebookfriendly.com/fan-fiction-websites).

Evans, Katy. "Daring Imaginarist Marissa Meyer."
Postdefiance.com, March 30, 2012. Retrieved
May 4, 2015 (http://postdefiance.com/
daring-imaginarist-marissa-meyer).

Fanbolt. "Exclusive Interview with Marissa Meyer of
'The Lunar Chronicles.'" August 7, 2014.
Retrieved May 6, 2015 (http://www.fanbolt.
com/40478/exclusive-interview-marissa-
meyer-lunar-chronicles).

Fowler, Tara. "Marissa Meyer talks 'Scarlet,' her
worries over 'Cinder' and a potential movie."
Posted January 18, 2015. Retrieved May 6,
2015 (http://www.ew.com/article/2013/02/14/
marissa-meyer-talks-scarlet-her-worries-over-
cinder-and-a-potential-movie-exclusive).

Fry, Erin. "Spring 2012 Flying Starts: Marissa Meyer."
Posted January 29, 2012. Retrieved April 30,
2015 (http://www.publishersweekly.com/pw/
by-topic/authors/profiles/article/52826-spring-
2012-flying-starts-marissa-meyer.html).

Graves, Caleb. "Exclusive Interview with Marissa
Meyer: 'Cress,' ending the 'Lunar Chronicles'
and future novels." Bibliofiend.com, October 3,
2013. Retrieved April 17, 2015 (http://biblio-
fiend.com/2013/10/03/
exclusive-interview-with-marissa-meyer-cress-
ending-the-lunar-chronicles-and-future-nov-
els/#).

Graves, Caleb. "Marissa Meyer announces new YA
novel 'Heartless.'" Bibliofiend.com, September
30, 2013. Retrieved May 5, 2015 (http://biblio-
fiend.com/2013/09/30/
marissa-meyer-announces-new-ya-novel-heart-
less/#).

Lamb, Joyce. "Interview: Marissa Meyer, author of
'Cress.'" USA Today, February 5, 2014.
Retrieved May 4, 2015 (http://www.usatoday.
com/story/happyeverafter/2014/02/05/
marissa-meyer-interview-cress/5219807).

Lodge, Sally. "Feiwel and Friends Rolls Out 'Cinder' in
High Style." Publishers Weekly, December 15,
2011. Retrieved May 4, 2015 (http://www.pub-
lishersweekly.com/pw/by-topic/childrens/
childrens-book-news/article/49873-feiwel-and-
friends-rolls-out-cinder-in-high-style.html).

Marissameyer.com. "Marissa Meyer: FAQ." Retrieved
     May 5, 2015 (http://www.marissameyer.com/faq).
Marissameyer.com. "From Idea to Finished, Step 1:
     Brainstorming & Research." September 4, 2014.
     Retrieved May 5, 2015 (http://www.marissa-
     meyer.com/blogtype/from-idea-to-finished-
     step-1-brainstorming-research).
Marissameyer.com. "From Idea to Finished, Step 2:
     The Outline." September 8, 2014. Retrieved May
     5, 2015 (http://www.marissameyer.com/blog-
     type/from-idea-to-finished-step-2-the-outline).
Marissameyer.com. "From Idea to Finished, Step 3:
     The First Draft." September 11, 2014. Retrieved
     May 5, 2015 (http://www.marissameyer.com/
     blogtype/
     from-idea-to-finished-step-3-the-first-draft).
Marissameyer.com. "From Idea to Finished, Step 4:
     Simmering Periods." September 15, 2014.
     Retrieved May 5, 2015 (http://www.marissa-
     meyer.com/blogtype/
     from-idea-to-finished-step-4-simmering-peri-
     ods).
Marissameyer.com. "From Idea to Finished, Step 5:
     The Second Draft." September 18, 2014.
     Retrieved May 5, 2015 (http://www.marissa-
     meyer.com/blogtype/
     from-idea-to-finished-step-5-the-second-draft).
Marissameyer.com. "From Idea to Finished, Step 6:
     Revisions." September 22, 2014. Retrieved May
     5, 2015 (http://www.marissameyer.com/blog-
     type/from-idea-to-finished-step-6-revisions).

Marissameyer.com. "From Idea to Finished, Step 7: Beta Readers & Final Revisions." September 25, 2014. Retrieved May 5, 2015. (http://www.marissameyer.com/blogtype/from-idea-to-finished-step-7-beta-readers-final-revisions).

Marissameyer.com. "From Idea to Finished, Step 8: Tweaking and Polishing." September 29, 2014. Retrieved May 5, 2015 (http://www.marissa-meyer.com/blogtype/from-idea-to-finished-step-8-tweaking-and-polishing).

Marissameyer.com. "From Idea to Finished, Step 9: The Publisher's Editorial Process." October 2, 2014. Retrieved May 5, 2015 (http://www.marissameyer.com/blogtype/from-idea-to-finished-step-9-the-publishers-editorial-process).

Reierson, Carrie. "Author, alum Marissa Meyer talks 'Sailor Moon' and 'Cinder.'" *Mast Media*, May 4, 2014. Retrieved April 17, 2015 (http://mastmedia.plu.edu/2014/05/04/author-alum-marissa-meyer-talks-sailor-moon-and-cinder).

Romney, Ginny. "Author Marissa Meyer blends sci-fi, fairy tales in companion tale to best-selling Lunar Chronicles series." *Deseret News*, January 23, 2015. Retrieved April 17, 2015 (http://www.deseretnews.com/article/865620239/Author-Marissa-Meyer-blends-sci-fi-fairy-tales-in-companion-tale-to-best-selling-Lunar-Chronicles.html?pg=all).

Sailor, Craig. "South Sound author Marissa Meyer reveals story of lunar queen in prequel." *The News Tribune*, January 22, 2015. Retrieved May 25, 2015 (http://www.thenewstribune. com/2015/01/22/3599675/find-what-lead-levana-to-her-evil.html).

Sailor, Craig. "Tacoma novelist hits it big with her futuristic story 'Cinder.'" *The News Tribune*, February 3, 2012. Retrieved April 17, 2015 (http://web.archive.org/web/20120603021128/ http://www.thenewstribune. com/2012/02/03/2010487/fairy-tale-meets-sci-fi. html).

Truitt, Brian. "Cover reveal, excerpt and Q&A: Marissa Meyer's 'Cress.'" *USA Today*, July 31, 2013. Retrieved May 6, 2015 (http://www.usatoday. com/story/life/books/2013/07/31/ cress-book-cover-excerpt-reveal/2600463).

Ward, Jean Marie. "The Lunar Chronicles Author— Marissa Meyer Interview: Meyer speaks about her work on The Lunar Chronicles – a series surrounding fairytales that have turned Science Fiction." *Buzzy Mag*, January 29, 2015. Retrieved May 5, 2015 (http://buzzymag.com/ lunar-chronicles-author-marissa-meyer-inter-view).

INDEX

ABOUT THE AUTHOR

Laura La Bella is the author of more than twenty-five nonfiction children's books. She is also an avid reader of young adult novels. Her favorites include *The Mortal Instruments* by Cassandra Clare and *The Vampire Academy* by Richelle Mead. La Bella lives in Rochester, New York, with her husband and two sons.

PHOTO CREDITS

Cover, p. 3 Triff/Shutterstock.com; p. 7 Danita Delimont/Gallo Images/Getty Images; p. 11 Shaun Egan/The Image Bank/Getty Images; p. 13 Julian Love/AWL Images/Getty Images; pp. 16-17 Sam Aronov/Shutterstock.com; pp. 18-19 Gregory Olsen/E+/Getty Images; p. 25 Alexandra Wyman/Getty Images; pp. 26-27 The Washington post/Getty Images; p. 31 Brent N. Clarke/FilmMagic/Getty Images; p. 33 Thomas Kuhlenbeck/Ikon Images/Getty Images; pp. 34-35 © iStock.com/MundusImages; pp. 40-41 © iStock.com/Maica; pp. 44-45 Maarten de Boer/Getty Images; pp. 48-49 Culture Club/Hulton Archive/Getty Images; p. 51 View Pictures/Universal Images Group/Getty Images; pp. 52-53 Patrick Aventurier/Gamma-Rapho/Getty Images; pp. 56-57 Anthony Pidgeon/Getty Images; pp. 60-61 Marianne Barcellona/The LIFE Images Collection/Getty Images; pp. 64-65 © iStock.com/scyther5; pp. 66-67 Francois Guillot/AFP/Getty Images; p. 68 Apic/Hulton Archive/Getty Images; p. 73 Chelsea Lauren/WireImage/Getty Images; p. 78 Print Collector/Hulton Archive/Getty Images; pp. 80-81 Bloomberg/Getty Images; pp. 84-85 Fort Worth Star-Telegram/Tribune News Service/Getty Images; cover, interior pages (book) © www.istockphoto.com/Andrzej Tokarski, (textured background) javarman/Shutterstock.com; interior pages (forest path) Elena Schweitzer/Shutterstock.com

Designer: Nicole Russo; Editor: Philip Wolny; Photo Researcher: Philip Wolny